Waves: Light and Sound

Light Waves

Robin Johnson and Douglas Hicton

LIGHTBOX
openlightbox.com

LIGHTBOX

Go to **www.openlightbox.com** and enter this book's unique code.

ACCESS CODE

LBXN6873

Lightbox is an all-inclusive digital solution for the teaching and learning of curriculum topics in an original, groundbreaking way. Lightbox is based on National Curriculum Standards.

OPTIMIZED FOR

- ✓ TABLETS
- ✓ WHITEBOARDS
- ✓ COMPUTERS
- ✓ AND MUCH MORE!

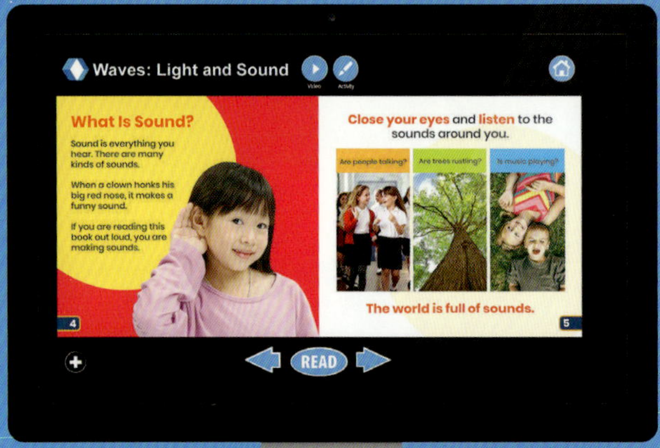

STANDARD FEATURES OF LIGHTBOX

 **AUDIO** High-quality narration using text-to-speech system

 **VIDEOS** Embedded high-definition video clips

 **ACTIVITIES** Printable PDFs that can be emailed and graded

 **WEBLINKS** Curated links to external, child-safe resources

 **SLIDESHOWS** Pictorial overviews of key concepts

 **INTERACTIVE MAPS** Interactive maps and aerial satellite imagery

 **QUIZZES** Ten multiple choice questions that are automatically graded and emailed for teacher assessment

 **KEY WORDS** Matching key concepts to their definitions

VIDEOS

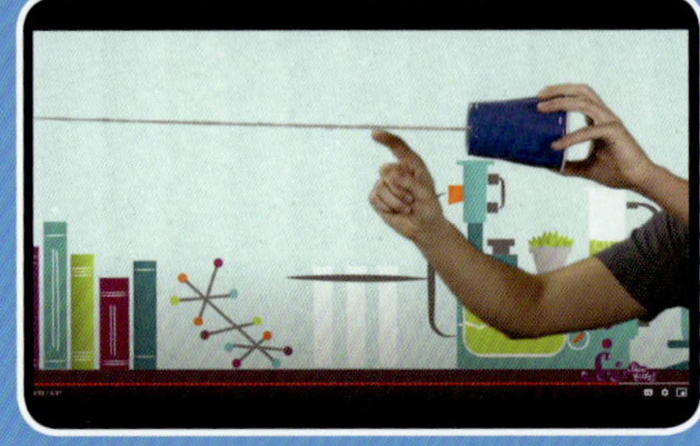

WEBLINKS

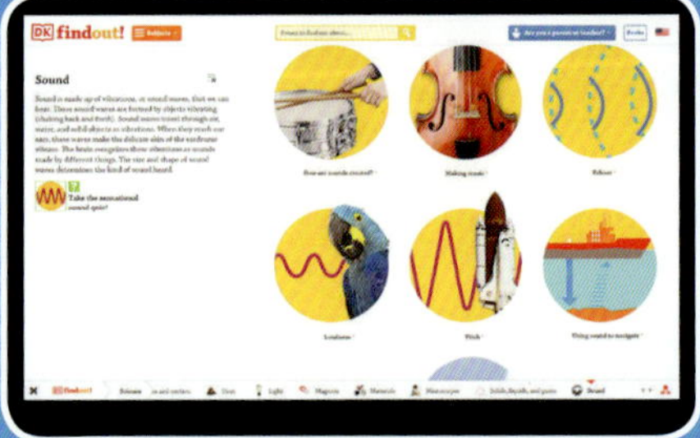

SLIDESHOWS

QUIZZES

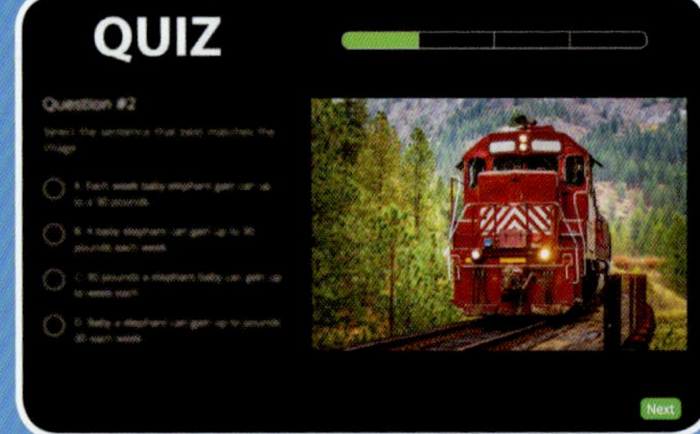

Light Waves

Contents

What Is Light?

Light is why we can see. You are reading this book because of light.

Some lights, like the Sun, are bright. Other lights, like night-lights, are dim.

Take time to notice how **light changes** through the **day**.

There is a light for every time of day.

We Need Light

Light shows us where we are. It also shows us where to go. Light helps us see what we need to do. Most tasks are impossible without it.

With no light, nothing would get made. Nobody could travel anywhere. Crops would die. We would no longer exist.

Light helps us **communicate** with each other.

Traffic lights tell us when to stop, go, or slow down. They keep us safe.

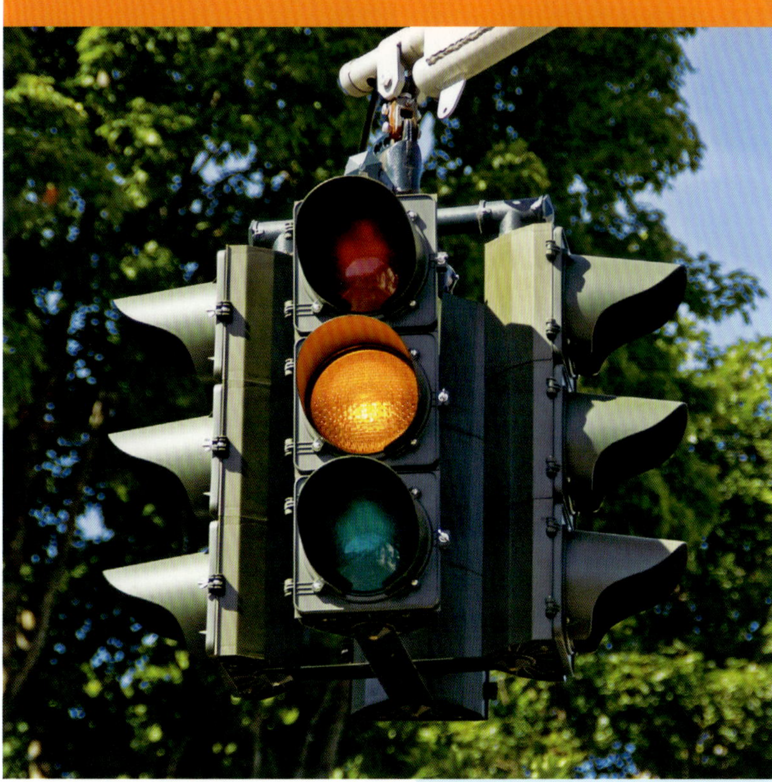

Lighthouses use light to communicate. They warn ships when they are close to shore.

Light in the Darkness

When the Sun goes down each day, everything is in darkness. You cannot see when there is no light. You use electric lights to help you see.

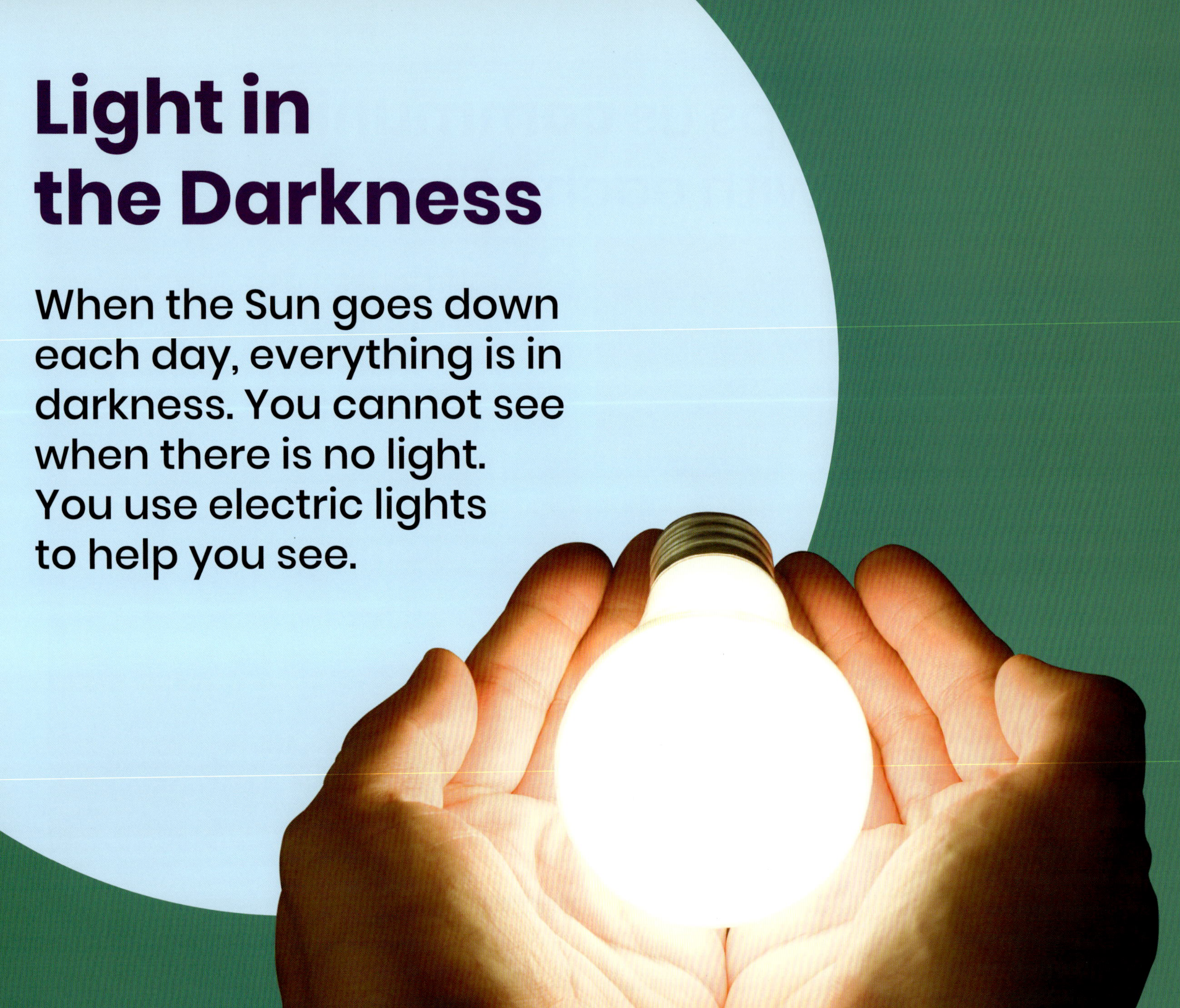

There is light even at **night**.

Light Is Energy

Energy is the power to do work. Some energy heats our homes, and some energy fuels our bodies. Light is a ray of energy. We once used candles and oil lamps for light. Today, we usually use electricity.

Have you ever seen lightning during a thunderstorm? Lightning is an example of electrical energy.

Lightning is **five times hotter** than the surface of the **Sun**.

Light from the Sun

The Sun is our main source of light. It is very powerful. The Sun is so hot and bright that its light can actually burn you. You should wear sunscreen to protect your skin. A big hat and sunglasses will protect your eyes.

Light and **heat** go together.

A candle flame makes light by making heat.

A light bulb is hot enough to cook food.

Hot coals glow with red light.

Light Waves

All sources of light make light waves. Light waves are rays of energy. You can see this energy.

Waves of different sizes make different colors. Red waves are long. Violet waves are short.

Alaska's Northern Lights shine best in the dark winter.

Some light **cannot** be **seen**.

Night vision goggles help you see in the dark. They let you see infrared light, which cannot be seen by your eyes.

Ultraviolet light rays are present in sunlight. You cannot see them, but you can see the sunburns they cause.

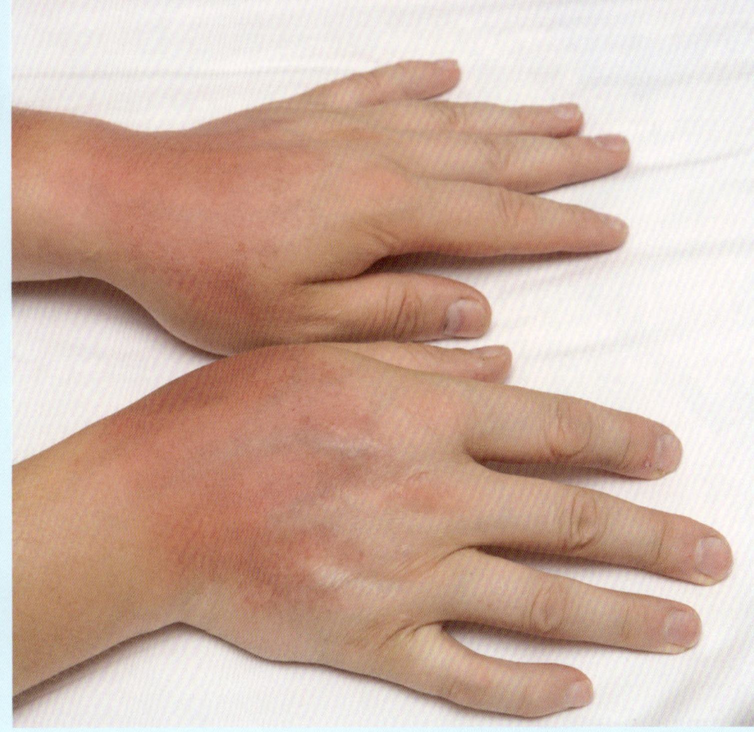

Light and Matter

Light waves travel in straight lines until they hit matter. Matter takes up space. It can be seen or touched.

Everything is made of matter. Your toys are matter. This book is matter. You are made of matter, too!

When you see something, you see how its matter reflects light. To reflect means to bounce off something.

The way light **bounces** changes how **we see ourselves.**

We are used to seeing ourselves backward. Look in a mirror. Compare what you see with a photograph of yourself. Does the photograph seem a bit strange?

Look at your reflection in a shiny spoon. Find out why it looks like you are standing on your head.

How Do We See?

The pupil is the black spot in the center of your eye. Light waves enter the eye through the pupil. The pupil grows or shrinks. This lets in more or less light.

The light hits the retina, which sends the image to the brain. The brain then translates it.

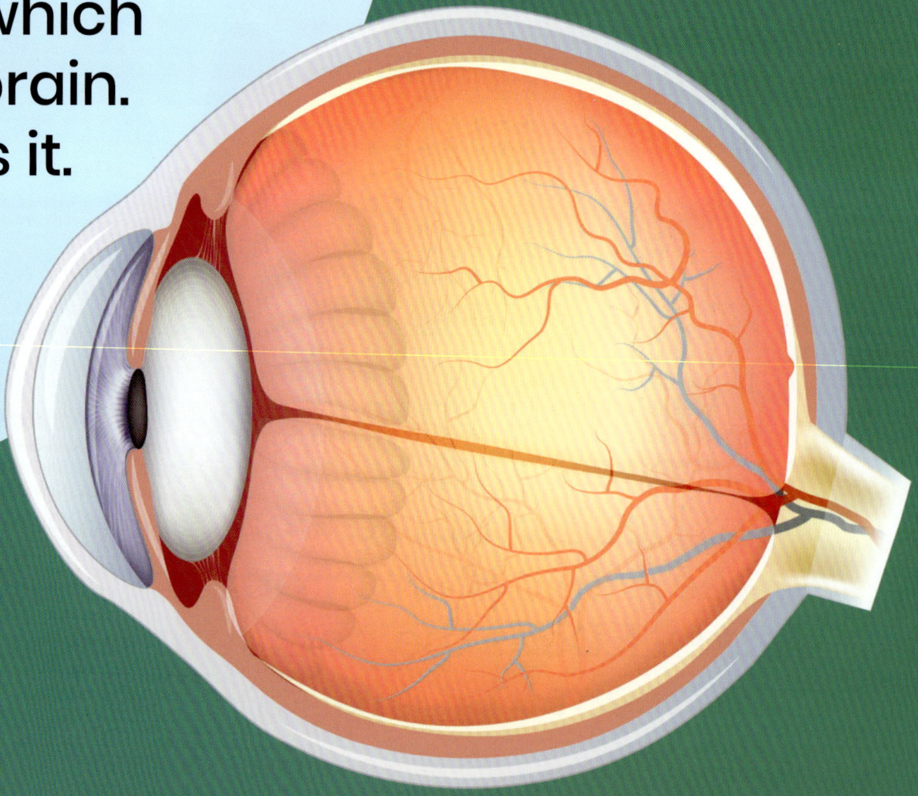

Retinas have **rod-shaped** and **cone-shaped** cells.

Rods help us see shapes. They work best in dim light.

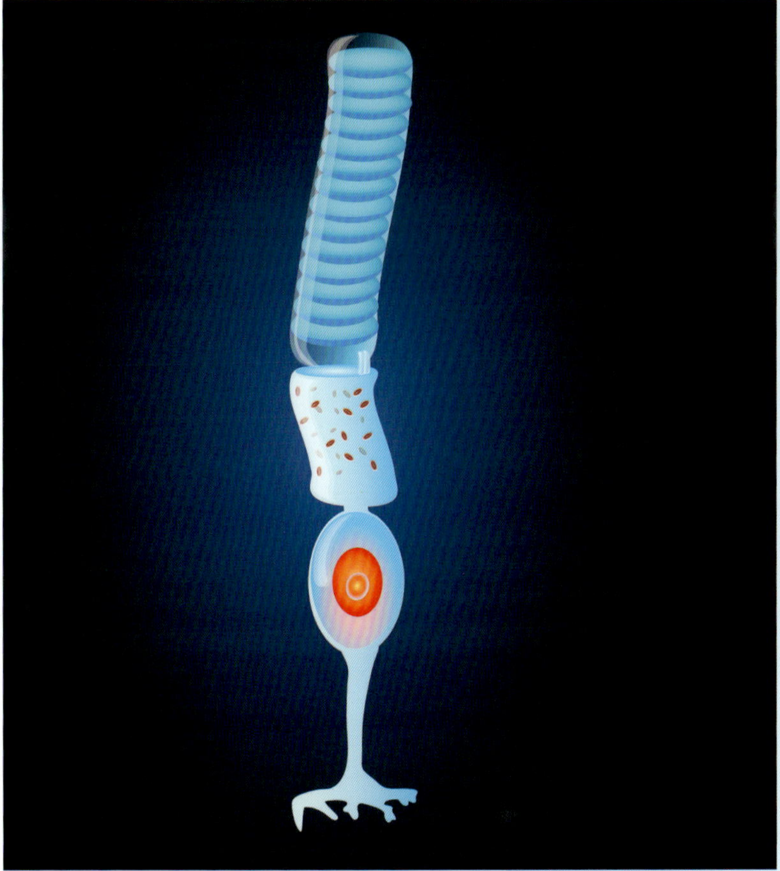

Cones give us color vision. We use them more in the daytime.

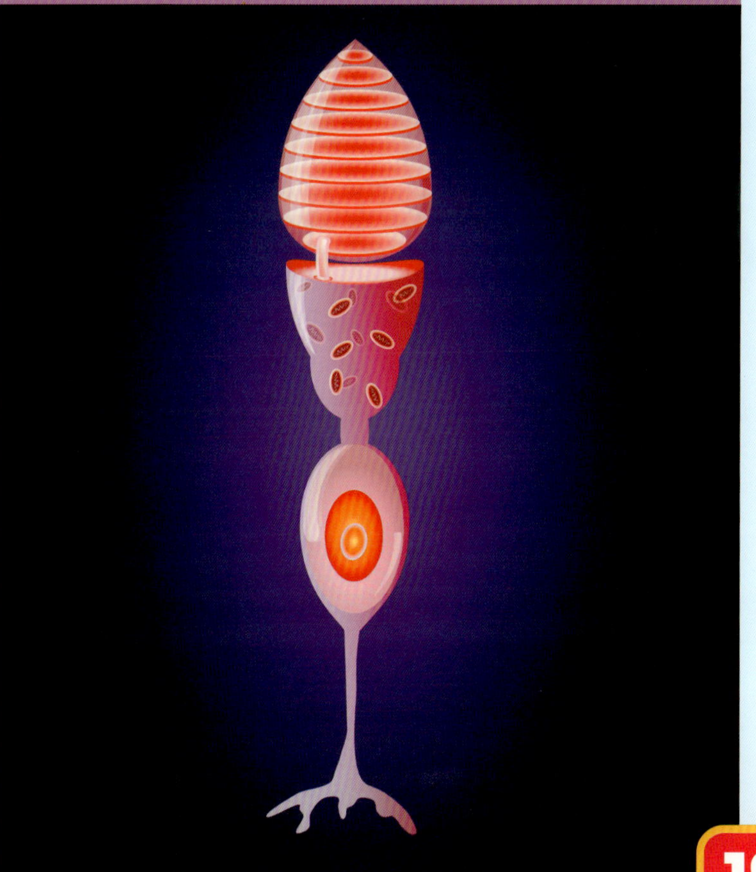

Communicating Without Light

Some people only see light and shadow. Others see nothing at all. These people are blind. Long ago, blind people could not read or write.

Louis Braille invented a system of writing for blind people. His system uses raised bumps. Fingertips read them as letters. The blind are also helped by audiobooks.

Louis Braille was blinded when he was **three years old**.

Activity

Make an Object Disappear

Every object has its own light wavelength. It disappears if its surroundings have the same wavelength. You can make a glass rod invisible. Just change its surroundings.

Supplies

Glass rod

Two glass jars or beakers

Water

Vegetable oil

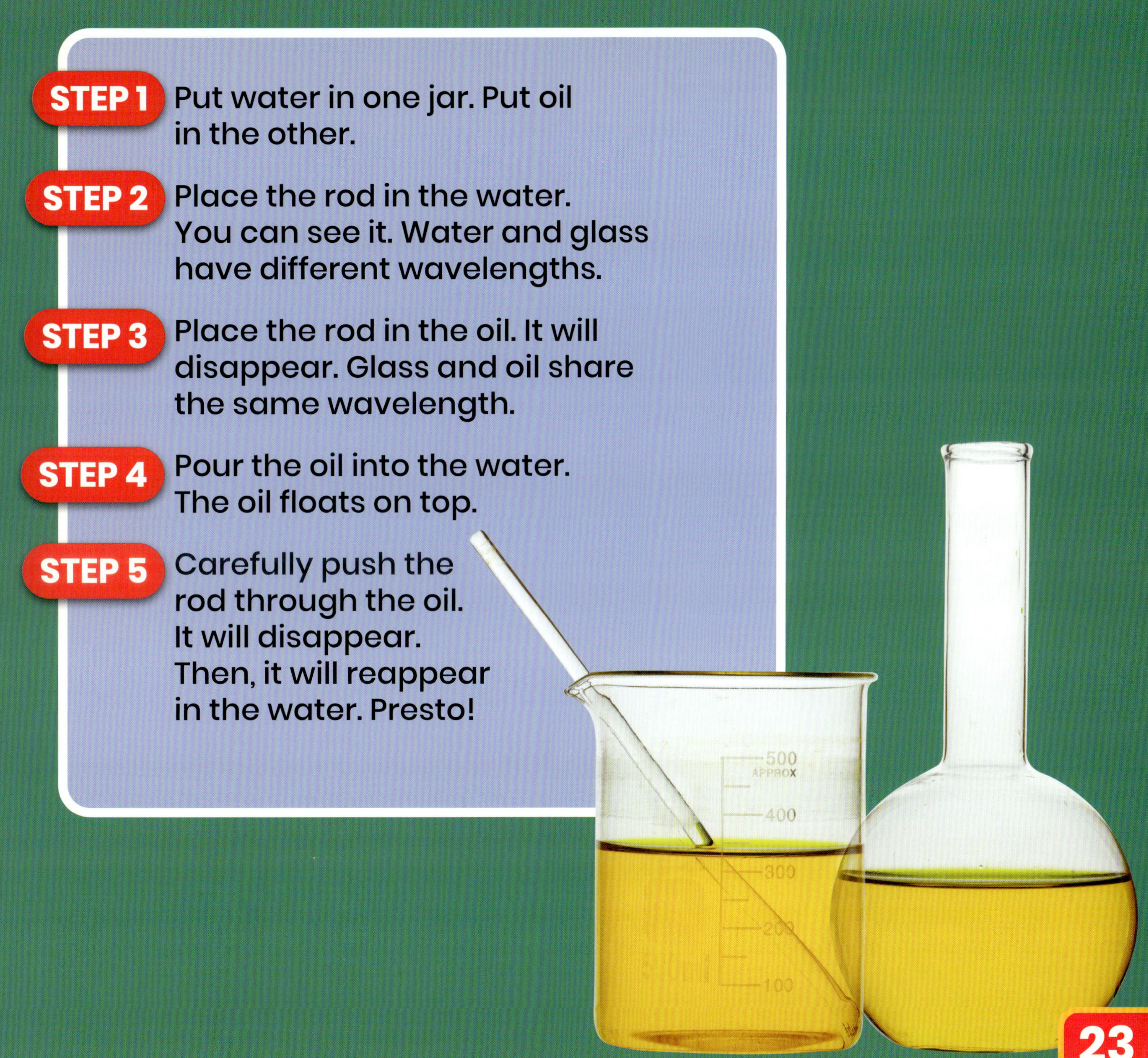

STEP 1 Put water in one jar. Put oil in the other.

STEP 2 Place the rod in the water. You can see it. Water and glass have different wavelengths.

STEP 3 Place the rod in the oil. It will disappear. Glass and oil share the same wavelength.

STEP 4 Pour the oil into the water. The oil floats on top.

STEP 5 Carefully push the rod through the oil. It will disappear. Then, it will reappear in the water. Presto!

KEY WORDS

Research has shown that as much as 65 percent of all written material published in English is made up of 300 words. These 300 words cannot be taught using pictures or learned by sounding them out. They must be recognized by sight. This book contains 125 common sight words to help young readers improve their reading fluency and comprehension. This book also teaches young readers several important content words, such as proper nouns. These words are paired with pictures to aid in learning and improve understanding.

Page	Sight Words First Appearance
4	are, because, book, can, is, light, like, of, other, see, some, the, this, we, what, why, you
5	a, and, changes, day, every, for, how, still, take, there, through, time, to
6	also, could, do, get, go, helps, it, made, most, need, no, shows, us, where, with, without, would
7	close, down, each, keep, or, stop, tell, they, use, when
8	in
9	at, even, night
10	an, example, have, homes, once, our, work
11	than
12	big, eyes, from, its, should, so, that, very, will, your
13	by, enough, food, makes, together
14	all, different, long
15	be, but, let, them, which
16	lines, means, off, something, too, until, up
17	does, find, head, look, on, out, seem, way
18	grows, more, then
19	give
20	as, his, letters, not, only, people, read, these, write
21	he, old, three, was, years

Page	Content Words First Appearance
4	night-lights, Sun
5	afternoon, evening, morning
6	crops, tasks
7	lighthouses, ships, shore, traffic lights
8	darkness, electric lights
9	campfire, fireflies, Moon
10	beam, bodies, candles, electricity, energy, lightning, oil lamps, power, thunderstorm
11	surface
12	hat, sunglasses, skin, sunscreen
13	coals, flame, heat, light bulb
14	Alaska, colors, light waves, Northern Lights, rays, winter
15	infrared light, night vision goggles, sunburns, sunlight, ultraviolet light
16	matter, space, toys
17	mirror, photograph, reflection, spoon
18	brain, image, pupil, retina
19	cells, color vision, cone, daytime, rod, shapes
20	audiobooks, blind, bumps, fingertips, Louis Braille, shadow, system

Published by Smartbook Media Inc.
14 Penn Plaza, 9th Floor New York, NY 10122
Website: www.openlightbox.com

Library of Congress Control Number: 2020937077

ISBN 978-1-5105-5402-3 (hardcover)
ISBN 978-1-5105-5403-0 (multi-user eBook)

Printed in Guangzhou, China
1 2 3 4 5 6 7 8 9 0 24 23 22 21 20

052020
110819

Project Coordinator: Priyanka Das
Designer: Jean Faye Marie Rodriguez

Every reasonable effort has been made to trace ownership and to obtain permission to reprint copyright material. The publisher would be pleased to have any errors or omissions brought to its attention so that they may be corrected in subsequent printings.

The publisher acknowledges Getty Images, iStock, and Shutterstock as the primary image suppliers for this title.

First published by Crabtree Publishing Company in 2014.